MANCHESTER United

Bill Day

Illustrated by Craig Warwick

Purnell

A PURNELL BOOK
Text © Bill Day 1988
Illustrations © Macdonald & Co (Publishers) Ltd 1988
First published in Great Britain in 1988
by Macdonald & Co (Publishers) Ltd
London & Sydney
A member of Maxwell Pergamon Publishing Corporation plc

Macdonald & Co (Publishers) Ltd
Greater London House
Hampstead Road
London NW1 7QX

British Library Cataloguing in Publication Data

Day, Bill
    Manchester United.
    1. England. Association football. Clubs:
    Manchester United Football Club, to 1986
    I. Title II. Series
    796.334'63'0942733

    ISBN 0-361-08492-7
    ISBN 0-361-68493-5 Pbk

Cover photograph: Colorsport

Typeset, printed and bound in Great Britain by
Hazell Watson & Viney Limited
Member of BPCC plc
Aylesbury, Bucks, England

Contents

Useful Addresses

Manchester United Football Club: Old Trafford, Warwick Road North, Manchester M16 ORA

Supporters' Club Information: Administrator: David Smith, c/o Club

There are many regional branches of the supporters' club. Write to the above person for details of the one nearest to you.

Manchester United Honours

First Division Champions: 1907–08, 1910–11, 1951–52, 1955–56, 1956–57, 1964–65, 1966–67

Second Division Champions: 1935–36, 1974–75

F.A. Cup Winners: 1909, 1948, 1963, 1977, 1983, 1985

European Cup Winners: 1968

MANCHESTER UNITED 1987–88 LEAGUE RECORD

Match	Date	Venue	Opponents	Result		Goalscorers
1	Aug 15	A	Southampton	D	2–2	Whiteside 2
2	19	H	Arsenal	D	0–0	
3	22	H	Watford	W	2–2	McGrath, McClair
4	29	A	Charlton Ath	W	3–1	McClair, Robson, McGrath
5	31	H	Chelsea	W	3–1	McClair, Strachan, Whiteside
6	Sept 5	A	Coventry C	D	0–0	
7	12	H	Newcastle U	D	2–2	Olsen, McClair (pen)
8	19	A	Everton	L	1–2	Whiteside
9	26	H	Tottenham H	W	1–0	McClair (pen)
10	Oct 3	A	Luton T	D	1–1	McClair
11	10	A	Sheffield W	W	4–2	Robson, McClair 2, Blackmore
12	17	H	Norwich C	W	2–1	Davenport, Robson
13	25	A	West Ham U	D	1–1	Gibson
14	31	H	Nottingham F	D	2–2	Robson, Whiteside
15	Nov 15	H	Liverpool	D	1–1	Whiteside
16	21	A	Wimbledon	L	1–2	Blackmore
17	Dec 5	A	QPR	W	2–0	Davenport, Robson
18	12	H	Oxford U	W	3–1	Strachan 2, Olsen
19	19	A	Portsmouth	W	2–1	Robson, McClair
20	26	A	Newcastle U	L	0–1	
21	28	H	Everton	W	2–1	McClair 2 (1 pen)
22	Jan 1	H	Charlton Ath	D	0–0	
23	2	A	Watford	W	1–0	McClair
24	16	H	Southampton	L	0–2	
25	24	A	Arsenal	W	2–1	Strachan, McClair
26	Feb 6	H	Coventry C	W	1–0	O'Brien
27	10	A	Derby Co	W	2–1	Whiteside, Strachan
28	13	A	Chelsea	W	2–1	Bruce, O'Brien
29	23	A	Tottenham H	D	1–1	McClair
30	Mar 5	A	Norwich C	L	0–1	
31	12	H	Sheffield W	W	4–1	Blackmore, McClair 2, Davenport
32	19	A	Nottingham F	D	0–0	
33	26	H	West Ham U	W	3–1	Strachan, Anderson, Robson
34	April 2	H	Derby	W	4–1	McClair 3, Gibson
35	4	A	Liverpool	D	3–3	Robson 2, Strachan
36	12	H	Luton T	W	3–0	McClair, Robson, Davenport
37	30	H	QPR	W	2–1	Bruce, Parker (og)
38	May 2	A	Oxford	W	2–0	Anderson, Strachan
39	7	H	Portsmouth	W	4–1	McClair 2 (1 pen), Davenport, Robson
40	9	H	Wimbledon	W	2–1	McClair 2 (1 pen)

Final League position: 2nd

Introduction

WHEN you visit Manchester United's magnificent Old Trafford stadium with its vast cantilever roof, be sure to go to the museum. Attracting almost 30,000 visitors every year, it contains an Aladdin's Cave of treasures from the club's glorious past. And in a place of honour you can see a fabulous replica of the European Cup, costing more than £10,000!

The world's most famous football club has commemorated its historic achievement in becoming the first Football League club to win the prestigious trophy by commissioning skilled craftsmen to produce a dazzling replica of the cup in silver and gold. The trophy is an exact copy of the Cup that was held aloft by Bobby Charlton at Wembley stadium, after United's stunning 4–1 victory over Benfica on 29 May 1968.

The European Cup represents the very pinnacle of United's trophy-winning exploits in their rise to stardom. Today, the club's players are among the highest paid footballers in

Europe; attendances are booming; there are supporters' clubs in a host of foreign countries; and United's prestige is the envy of clubs all over the world. From Brisbane to Buenos Aires, from Mexico City to Moscow, and from Washington to Wellington, England captain Bryan Robson and his Manchester United team-mates are household names.

It is hard to believe that the Rolls-Royce club of British football was once almost bankrupt: its team had to get changed in a pub, and life was a constant battle for survival – saved at one point only by the wanderlust of a St Bernard dog . . .

This book tells the story of Manchester United's rise from humble beginnings in the suburbs of the great northern city, to their position as just about the most famous club side in the world.

Chapter One

Early Days

THE age of steam was just gathering momentum as a popular form of travel in late Victorian times. In Manchester, a group of railway workers brightened their lunchbreaks with kickabouts in the depot yard behind the wagon works at Newton Heath.

The matches became so popular among the workforce in this grimy corner of a Manchester suburb that the Lancashire and Yorkshire Railway formed a team. Known as Newton Heath Football Club, the team played their first game at North Road in 1878, joined the Football League in 1892, and on an historic day in 1902 the club became known as Manchester United.

In the early days, as Newton Heath or the 'Heathens', the players were unpaid amateurs, changing in a pub in the Oldham Road known as The Three Crowns. Many of the team would come straight from a shift at the works to pull green-and-gold shirts over faces blackened by hours of toil. They worked in a factory turning out the rolling stock that carried passengers and goods across Britain's fast-growing rail network.

The Doughty brothers, Roger and Jack, were early heroes for Newton Heath. Goal-keepers were given no protection by referees in those days, and on many occasions the brawny Jack Doughty, known as 'The Crasher', would send a keeper sprawling in his penalty area. Jack had the honour of scoring the 'Heathens' first goal in their first game in September 1888.

Going professional

In 1892 the 'Heathens' were admitted to the Football League. They were now professional, becoming a Limited Company with a full-time secretary. They hammered Walsall to a record 14–0 defeat in 1894–95, and when the match was declared void, beat them again 9–0.

A lot of fun of the early kickabouts had given way to the deadly serious business of running a full-time club. Newton Heath was desperately hard up. The team struggled to pay six shillings a week – worth 30p today – for the use of a house as their headquarters. The Clergy of Manchester, owners of their North Road enclosure, refused to allow the club to charge admission to matches. So, Newton Heath became probably the first and only professional club with *no* income.

However, the enthusiasm for football in the big northern city was so feverish that Newton Heath took little time setting up home in Bank Street, Clayton, during 1893–94. The ground was a fine one, spoiled only by the wooden hut in which the team changed. Many observers of that period reckon that the move to Clayton was worth a goal start for Newton Heath. Thick black smoke, belching from chimneys of a chemical works next to the ground, polluted the air and choked the unprepared opposition!

Newton Heath spent its first two seasons in the First Division, followed by eight in the Second Division. James M'Naught was the Bryan Robson of that era. They called him the 'little wonder', a tribute to his dazzling skills and silky passes to forwards such as Joe Cassidy, whose rocket shooting served Celtic and Middlesbrough also. Caesar Jenkins was another star of the team. Big and powerful, he had loads of talent – and a mouth to match.

New players joined Newton Heath from all parts of the country. Supporters would go to the local railway station to welcome any newcomer as he stepped off the train.

The players were good, and the football was good, but the business side of the club was a disaster . . .

A St Bernard to the rescue

It came as no surprise in 1902 when local newspapers warned that the club was bankrupt. Harry Stafford, a former captain, ran a four-day bazaar to raise funds. Shoppers were invited to buy season tickets to the big event, costing three shillings and sixpence.

Mancunians flocked to St James's Hall in Manchester's busy Oxford Street, but as they flooded through the entrance, Harry's pet St Bernard dog was wandering through an exit door with a collecting box swinging from her collar. Tired, hungry, and lost at nightfall, the St Bernard was taken in by the landlord of a city pub, one of several inns owned by J. H. Davies, who was one of Manchester's biggest businessmen.

The dog was returned to Harry Stafford, while Mr Davies was so impressed by Harry's fund raising efforts that he set up a consortium to pay off the Heath's debts of £2000. Furthermore, he was so pleased with his rescue act that he helped found a new club. Manchester United was born on 28 April, 1902.

The new team

Ernest Mangnall, well known for his Charlie Chaplin moustache and straw hat, was appointed the first manager of the new club in September 1903. His knowledge and coaching skills helped Charlie Roberts become the first United player to represent England in 1905.

In 1906 Mangnall made a sensational move to land the Welsh wizard Billy Meredith, who was banned from playing at the time for big city rivals Manchester City because of his involvement in a bribe scandal. Mangnall got his man for a bargain £500, even though Meredith was still suspended. And the new United supremo was to sign four more City players, all of them suffering the disgrace of suspension for their part in an illegal payments racket.

Mangnall's United won their first Championship in 1907–08, powering to the title on the brilliance of the flying winger Meredith, who went on to win 48 caps for Wales over 25 golden years.

Adopting a fan's pet goat as mascot, United won the F.A. Cup in 1909, beating Bristol City 1–0 at Crystal Palace through a goal from Sandy Turnbull. In 1910–11 the club won the First Division title again.

Old Trafford in the wars

But the Championship crown took almost secondary importance to a building that was rising from land on the Stretford side of the busy Manchester Ship Canal. It cost £60,000 and was called Old Trafford stadium. No football ground in the world, not even the Azteca in Mexico City, the Bernabau in Madrid, or Wembley itself was to offer a more electric crowd atmosphere than Old Trafford was to produce over the next 80 years.

Sandy Turnbull immortalised his name in United folklore by scoring the first goal in the new stadium against Liverpool in 1910. His goals were a considerable source of inspiration to poets of that era:

> *The ball was on the bound,*
> *And your boot was safe and sound,*
> *When the net your great shot found,*
> *Champion Sandy.*

The First World War robbed United of the heroic Turnbull. He died at Arras, serving bravely with the Manchester Regiment.

United could not recover their winning formula when peacetime resumed. They rose and fell between the First and Second Divisions as if controlled by a yo-yo expert. The long-forgotten cloud of bankruptcy threatened again. The club became a national joke, and a ready target for the spiteful humour of seaside pier comedians.

But as J. H. Davies' trusty lieutenant, Ernest Mangnall, had emerged to save United in the early days, so James Gibson (whose son Alan became Vice-President of the club in the 1980s) arrived to rescue the club.

The country was in turmoil in those dark days of the early 1930s and no group of men were worse off than the United team. When Gibson heard that some players could not afford a meal for Christmas Day, he gave them cash from his own pocket.

United was back in the Second Division at the end of the 1930–31 season, relegated for the third time. Three seasons later the club nearly slid into the Third Division, which would almost certainly have robbed it of any hope of achieving the greatness that was to come at the end of the Second World War. It avoided relegation by a point after beating Millwall 2–0. The winning and losing sequence received a bad press on the back pages of the national papers – as a man named Adolph Hitler began to make news on the front.

Before long the German Führer's bombs were being off-loaded from aircraft over England. A string of them fell on Manchester on the night of 11 March, 1941. The main stand at Old Trafford was demolished; the ground was an inferno; and the pitch on which Turnbull and company had thrilled thousands was blitzed. It would need a miracle for Manchester United to recover from that catastrophic blow to the club's fortunes.

Chapter Two

Busby Rules

THE main stand at Old Trafford had been blown apart. Only a handful of players were young enough to meet the demands of the First Division. Manchester United was £15,000 in debt. It needed a miracle to revive the club – and a messiah was on hand to lead Manchester United from the depths of post-war depression to a position of power with a following across the world.

Matt Busby turned down a coaching offer from Liverpool, and the chance to become manager of Ayr United, or assistant manager at Reading. He chose instead to become Manchester United's first 'track-suit' manager.

Only 35, the quiet, modest Busby took over from Scott Duncan, an autocratic United manager who wore a suit, a red rose in his buttonhole, and sent a shiver of apprehension through staff every time he spoke.

Calm, friendly, and ambitious, Busby was Duncan's opposite. Ever present at the training ground, he would run around with the

Matt Busby, Manager of Manchester United from 1945 to 1969.

same boyish enthusiasm he had paraded in his playing days at Liverpool and Manchester City. Busby's mud-caked tracksuit had to be sent to the laundry after most of the rigorous training sessions, but he soon earned the respect of coaching staff and players. He became a friendly dictator, possibly the Football League's first Total Manager, in charge of every aspect of club affairs.

The start of a golden reign

Busby knew from the outset that the team he inherited would never be good enough to enable him to fulfil his dreams of making Manchester United the best club in the land. His first signing was Jimmy Murphy, who became assistant manager. Murphy had impressed Busby in wartime by the way he handled Army footballers in Italy.

Busby's determination to run the playing side of the club as he wanted was illustrated by his angry exchange with Chairman James Gibson, who insisted Matt sign a Newcastle player. Busby refused and the Chairman stormed out of their meeting, only to return a few minutes later to apologise. Busby recalled later: 'I thought he would have a fit. He brandished his stick until I thought he would hit me.'

In another brush with authority, Busby told a director to get lost when the official tried to offer some advice on playing tactics. 'I run this club, not you,' Busby insisted.

From then on there was only one man in charge of the team – Matt Busby. He signed Jimmy Delaney from Celtic for £4000 to pull off one of the most successful transfers in United history. Critics complained that the 32-year-old Scottish winger was too old, but when Manchester United came runners-up to Liverpool for the title at the end of the 1946–47 season, Delaney was a firm favourite with the supporters.

That post-war team, using Manchester City's Maine Road ground as headquarters until Old Trafford was re-built, had all the class and style that Busby was to instil in the teams he produced in a golden management reign stretching from 1945–69.

The post-war team contained Johnny Carey, a Dubliner, who made 29 appearances for the Republic of Ireland in an outstanding career interrupted by war. More versatile even than today's hero Bryan Robson, Carey played in every position except goalkeeper in his 256 appearances for United after the war.

Allenby Chilton was a tall, commanding figure at the heart of United's defence and a key man in the post-war period. Busby picked him for 352 matches before the South Hylton born centre-half moved to Grimsby in 1955.

Busby moved inside-forward John Aston

to defence, to forge one of the League's finest full-back pairings with Carey, who captained the team.

The attack was led by England stars Stan Pearson and Jack Rowley, who scored almost 300 goals between them. Busby was warned he would never tame the temperamental Rowley, a lethal goal-poacher even from 40 metres range. 'I never had one moment's trouble with Rowley,' said Busby.

The post-war United spent more time attacking than defending, but if the opposition was lucky enough to find an opening, Jack Crompton's agility and safe handling in goal was equal to the call for duty. Not the tallest goalkeeper in the League, Crompton was a regular first-teamer from 1946–55.

'No player was ever fitter than Jack Crompton, or a greater clubman,' says Busby.

Busby was unsuccessful in three determined attempts to sign Frank Swift, the legendary Manchester City and England goalkeeper whom he had befriended in his Army days. His efforts to sign big Swifty were fiercely contested by the rival City management.

The Club's rising fortunes

The 1947–48 season saw an improving Manchester United, despite their obvious difficulties in having to share the Maine Road ground until 1949. The club finished second in the League and won the F.A. Cup for the first time since 1909.

Shrewd judges reckon the Manchester United forward line that destroyed the highly fancied Blackpool 4–2 at Wembley was the best League club attack in history. Delaney, Morris, Rowley, Pearson, and Mitten played like a dream machine. They overcame their disappointment at having conceded a hotly disputed penalty when Chilton was alleged to have tripped Stan Mortensen (newsreel proved the referee wrong), and went on to thrash Blackpool in one of the finest post-war Finals on record.

This was United's greatest hour as their fans celebrated breathtaking goals by Rowley (2), Pearson and John Anderson.

Manchester United protected a secret that day that remained with the club for the next 30 years. In 1978, the year United celebrated their centenary, goalkeeper Jack Crompton revealed that 48 hours before his Wembley appearance he was under an anaesthetic on an operating theatre table suffering from an abscess of the spine. 'On the morning of the game I had a short training session and it was pretty painful,' recalls Crompton. 'What an exciting match. The newspapers called it a classic. My injury was one of the best kept secrets in football.'

Manchester United would not repeat the mastery of that Wembley performance for several years. They were Championship runners-up to Portsmouth the following season and reached the F.A. Cup semi-finals. In 1949–50 they came fourth in the table, second in 1950–51, and finally in 1951–52 clinched their first title since the 1910–11 season.

Johnny Morris, a vital cog in the 1948 team, had joined Derby for £25,000. John Berry, a £25,000 recruit from Birmingham City, had restored sharpness to the flanks following the decline of the magnificent veteran Jimmy Delaney. Skipper Johnny Carey's hold on the Championship trophy after a Jack Rowley hat-trick had destroyed their main rivals, Arsenal, 6–1 at Old Trafford, was to prove a watershed in the great northern club's post-war history.

The Busby Babes
Busby decided that the time had come to break up the team. He wanted to build his *own* team, while not forgetting that he had inherited many of the stars who steered United to success after the war. He wanted the best young players available. The Busby Babes, soon to win acclaim all over Europe, were about to be baptized.

The first to emerge was Roger Byrne, a fast

winger converted to full-back as replacement for Aston. Byrne was one of a new breed of full-back favoured at the time, slim and fast, who could defend and then attack. The big, often overweight, ponderous type of full-back was in decline.

Joe Mercer, a close friend of Busby who had become one of Britain's greatest players in an outstanding career at Everton and Arsenal, and who later managed Coventry and Manchester City, played an important part in the birth of the 'Babes'.

On duty as coach to England Schoolboys, he was dazzled by the promise of a youngster from Dudley in Worcestershire by the name of Duncan Edwards. Mercer overheard Edwards say 'I'd love to join United,' and without hesitation Mercer told Busby he would be mad not to sign the burly teenager. 'At 15, he was a man already,' says Busby, who beat off a host of League clubs for Big Dunc's signature. 'He looked like a man. He played like a man.'

Wilf McGuinness, one of the Busby Babes who played alongside Edwards, described his team-mate in these terms: 'He was the complete player. Duncan could do everything, run, jump, shoot, beat opponents, and he was strong, so strong.'

Edwards' rise from boot-cleaning duties to the full England team in three years has

**Duncan Edwards, outstanding even amongst
the famous Busby Babes.**

earned him a golden chapter in the chronicles of football history. You can read about him on pages 73–5.

The Babes become legend

The Babes were beginning to buzz. Busby and his assistant Murphy camped out in a Barnsley pub for two days in a cloak-and-dagger mission to sign Tommy Taylor, a 20-year-old striker with thunder in his boots. Barnsley wanted £30,000 – only £4000 less than the British record – and Busby's fear that the price on Taylor's head would distress the young striker persuaded the two clubs to settle for £29,999.

Taylor arrived by train from Barnsley. His only luggage was a pair of football boots stuffed in his pockets! Two months later, he had won his first England cap after scoring seven goals in his first 13 League games for United.

The Busby Babes finished eighth in the League in 1953. A year later they came fourth, and in 1955 finished fifth. In 1955–56 and 1956–57 they stormed to two successive League titles. The nucleus of that brilliant young team comprised: goalkeeper Ray Wood, Billy Foulkes, Eddie Colman, Jackie Blanchflower, Mark Jones, Liam Whelan, Dennis Viollet, David Pegg, Bobby Charlton,

Roger Byrne, Tommy Taylor and Duncan Edwards.

The prize for winning the title in 1956 was entry to European competition for the first time. The European Champion Clubs' Cup (European Cup) was beginning to blossom after its inauguration in 1955. Chelsea, operating on Football League advice, had turned down an opportunity to become England's first entry, but United grabbed a chance to perform a unique treble – the European Cup, F.A. Cup, and League title.

Anderlecht, the Belgian champions, were United's first opponents in Europe. Tommy Taylor and Dennis Viollet destroyed them in a 2–0 defeat in Belgium. The second-leg in Manchester has never been forgotten. This time United won 10–0, Viollet scoring four, Taylor a hat-trick.

Borussia Dortmund, Honved and then Bilbao were swept aside by the rampaging Babes. Who could beat them? Real Madrid, the outstanding club team of that era, were equal to the task, beating United in the semi-finals.

The Babes' dream of pulling off a treble had collapsed, but Wembley beckoned in a 1957 F.A. Cup Final appearance against Aston Villa. United's hopes of winning lasted just six minutes until Peter McParland, Villa's Irish-born winger, charged goalkeeper

Wood, who was taken off with a fractured cheekbone. In those days before substitutes, Jackie Blanchflower pulled on the goal-keeper's jersey, and, spurred by a Tommy Taylor goal, United survived until the last half hour when McParland, booed every time he touched the ball, scored twice to sink the Babes.

No European trophy; no Cup; the Babes (average age just 21) had to settle for their second successive Championship.

With only Roger Byrne and Johnny Berry surviving from the 1952 title-winning team, the Busby Babes had become a legend.

The world weeps

The 1957–58 season was launched on a wave of enthusiasm. It was to end in tragedy.

Real Madrid made a futile bid to lure Busby to Spain as the United manager spoke optimistically of winning a third successive Championship. United thrashed deadly rivals Manchester City 4–1 in a bright start to the season; but wavered as Christmas approached, losing to Bolton by a 6–0 margin. Busby, never afraid to wave his cheque-book, strengthened the defence by signing Northern Ireland goalkeeper Harry Gregg from Doncaster Rovers for £25,000.

The club's exploits in Europe were in sharp contrast to its League form. It thrashed

Shamrock Rovers and overcame Dukla Prague 3–1 on aggregate, to win a place in a European Cup quarter-final tie against Red Star Belgrade.

The club then recovered its League form, and two stunning goals by a young Bobby Charlton and Eddie Colman gave the Babes a 2–1 first leg lead over Red Star at Old Trafford. Warmed by a 5–4 victory at Arsenal, in which Edwards had powered a goal, the Babes flew to Yugoslavia for the second leg. Brilliant goals by Charlton (2) and Viollet saw the Babes to victory in Belgrade, winning through to a semi-final tie against AC Milan.

The Babes were in high spirits when their Elizabethan aircraft gathered speed for take-off for the return journey on a slush covered runway at Munich on 6 February 1958.

Its tyres never left the icebound tarmac. Instead of taking off, the aircraft sped through landing lights, an airport fence, and into a house 250 yards from the runway.

Roger Byrne, Geoff Bent, Eddie Colman, Mark Jones, David Pegg, Tommy Taylor and Liam Whelan died. Duncan Edwards fought against injuries but died a fortnight later in hospital. John Berry and Jackie Blanchflower never played again. Ken Morgans, Albert Scanlon, Dennis Viollet, Ray Wood, and Matt Busby were injured.

The United secretary Walter Crickner

died, as did club coaches Tom Curry and Bert Whalley. Eight journalists were killed also, including Frank Swift.

In less than a minute the Busby Babes were no more and the heart had been torn out of the England team by the loss of Byrne, Taylor and Edwards, who already owned 18 caps.

'The world wept for Manchester United. My life had been spared but I wanted to die,' said Busby in a vivid account of the nightmare in which 23 people died.

The saddest season

Fate had dealt assistant manager Jimmy Murphy a lucky break. His appointment as Wales' manager meant that he missed the trip to Belgrade and it fell upon him to take charge of a decimated United squad for the rest of the season.

Huge crowds of 60,000 or more packed into Old Trafford to support Murphy's patchwork team made up of old heads, unknowns, reserves, and regular first teamers like Harry Gregg, Billy Foulkes and the emerging Charlton.

How the team reached the 1958 F.A. Cup Final on the crest of emotional support is one of football's happiest stories. They were beaten 2–0 by Bolton Wanderers with Matt Busby watching from the Wembley stands.

In the European Cup semi-final, Dennis

Viollet and Ernie Taylor, the England and Blackpool forward brought in to serve United in their emergency, scored goals to give United a 2–1 victory over AC Milan at Old Trafford. But the Italians showed no room for sentiment. They flogged United 4–0 in Milan, and cut short the club's European dream at the end of the most tragic season in Football League history.

The game must go on . . .

Busby, 13 years into his reign, had to build a third team. He broke the British transfer record to buy Sheffield Wednesday's cultured forward Albert Quixall for £45,000. Noel Cantwell, the Arsenal striker David Herd, and the Young England midfield player Maurice Setters arrived, and in August 1962 Busby pulled off his greatest transfer coup when he persuaded Denis Law to join from Torino for £115,000. The spring-heeled Scot scored 29 goals in the 1962–63 season, some of his goals made by Pat Crerand, a Scottish international midfield recruit from Celtic.

Manchester United reached their first F.A. Cup Final for five years, beating Leicester City 3–1 with two goals from David Herd and one from Denis Law.

By the start of the 1963–64 campaign a spindly-legged 17-year-old from Belfast was

Denis Law – 'The King' of Old Trafford.

beginning to make an impact in United's reserves. His name? George Best.

The club's Irish scout had dubbed Best a 'genius', and soon after making his début in September 1964, United's followers knew what all the talk was about.

Law, Best and Charlton went together like Little and Large. United won the Championship in 1965, again in 1967, and reached the European Cup semi-finals in 1965–66.

Matt Busby had yet to achieve one ambition – to win the European Cup. Manchester United, strengthened by the arrival of £60,000 Chelsea goalkeeper Alex Stepney, reached the European Cup Final in 1968 after beating the mighty Real Madrid in the semis. Now came Busby's finest hour, 10 years after his crippled body had fought for life in a Munich hospital. A capacity 100,000 Wembley crowd watched United thrash Benfica 4–1 in extra-time in an unforgettable European Cup Final.

Memorable goals by Bobby Charlton (two), Best and Brian Kidd, a powerful young striker from United's nursery of stars, did the damage.

Matt Busby was made Manager of the Year. Manchester United's supporters would have made him Manager of the Century, given half a chance! Busby was so overcome with pride and emotion at the celebration banquet that he allowed his Manager of the Year cheque for £1000 to slip from his pocket. 'I think this belongs to you, sir,' said a waiter, thrusting the cheque into Busby's hands.

The Manchester United boss was in joyous but thoughtful mood that historic night. He knew that part of the glory his team had achieved in Europe belonged to that pioneering Babes side, who had blazed a trail in Europe that the current team had explored so successfully a decade later. Matt Busby thought of a snow-covered runway; he thought of big Duncan Edwards; and he wept in the privacy of his hotel room.

In 1969 the Great Man retired from team affairs to become general manager at Old Trafford. A new era was about to dawn.

Chapter Three

United in Trouble

BY the time Matt Busby retired from the hot-seat after 23 years in charge of playing affairs at Old Trafford, his teams had won five League Championships, won the F.A. Cup twice, reached a Wembley Final on two other occasions, and won the European Cup.

By any standards it was a remarkable achievement. As he said at the time: 'Manchester United has not just become a football club. It has become a world famous organisation . . .'

It needed a BIG man to take over the reigns. Possible replacements were Don Revie, doing well at Leeds United; Jock Stein, mastermind behind Celtic's success in Europe; Ken Furphy, a bright young boss of Third Division Watford; Noel Cantwell, Coventry manager and former Old Trafford favourite; Malcolm Allison, junior partner of a joint-management team at Manchester City with Joe Mercer; and Brian Clough, then Manager of Derby County.

'Wilf' McGuinness

United shook the football world when they offered Wilf McGuinness the job. Forced into retirement with a broken leg, McGuinness, one of the Busby Babes who roomed with the late Duncan Edwards, was appointed in June 1969. His title was Team Manager, with Sir Matt – he had been knighted – maintaining overall control as chief of the playing staff. The older players referred to McGuinness as 'Wilf' and Sir Matt as 'Boss'.

McGuinness's appointment was a mistake that was to cause Manchester United a great deal of hardship over the next few years. McGuinness was one of the most honest and hard-working members of the backroom staff, first as player and then as part of the coaching outfit, but he could not handle his promotion from being 'one of the lads' to the man in charge.

He found it difficult to boss players he had grown up with in the youth team. Some tough decisions were not being made, and United's younger players were pressing for places on the first team that were occupied by some legendary names. When he did make decisions, McGuinness sometimes went wildly over the top. On one occasion he dropped both Denis Law and Bobby Charlton, two of the world's great talents. Sir Matt Busby remarked later: 'I did not agree with Wilf's dropping of Bobby Charlton and Denis Law on the same day. I do not wish to say that I would not have dropped Bobby or Denis or anybody else if I thought it was the right thing to do. I did not think it was the right time to do it.'

Part of Wilf's problem was that he had grown up in the shadow of United greats, such as Charlton, Law, Best, Crerand, Foulkes and Stiles. His appointment begged the question: 'Wilf who?'. He did fairly well in his first season in charge, steering Manchester United to the F.A. Cup semi-finals and to eighth place in the First Division. But the 1970–71 season was to expose the cracks that had been appearing since his appointment.

By December the 'Red Devils' had won only five of the 19 League games they had played, and attendances were dipping alarmingly. McGuinness's days were numbered when deadly rivals Manchester City humiliated United 4–1 at Old Trafford. A few weeks later McGuinness was sacked and asked to take charge of the second team.

Stormy Days

Again, Manchester United struggled to find a suitable recruit. Sir Matt ran playing affairs until the summer of 1971, when a softly-spoken Irishman named Frank O'Farrell left

Leicester City for Old Trafford after leading the Filbert Street club to the Second Division Championship. He had a baptism of fire when United slumped to a shock Watney Cup defeat against Halifax at the start of the 1971–72 season, but come Christmas, United were top of the First Division and the fans were loving it. Wizard winger Best had scored 14 goals and Law 12, some of their efforts carved from nothing. The defence was suspect but Alex Stepney was in peak form in goal, compensating for some of the mistakes being made in front of him.

The New Year brought a switchback in fortunes, the winning turning to a losing streak that saw the club lose seven League matches on the trot. More gravely for O'Farrell, Best, arguably the best player in Europe, was beginning to show the first signs of rebellious behaviour that was to damage and finally destroy his brilliant career.

Best missed a week's training in January 1972 and was promptly dropped, fined and ordered to leave his new house in Bramhall and take 'digs' where his lifestyle could be supervised. Best was such a public figure in those days that coach parties would make sight-seeing trips to his home. The superstar felt trapped, as if he lived in a goldfish bowl. He found an escape from the public in the nightclubs of Manchester, where drink and

George Best – a player with an astonishing, but sadly short, career.

girls were frequent companions. He was told he would be shot while playing for Manchester United at Newcastle. The threat came from a man claiming to represent the IRA. A letter signed 'The Striker' threatened a knife in the back, and the Best household was kept under surveillance by the police.

Best returned to Old Trafford to destroy Southampton in a third-round F.A. Cup replay, but his relationship with O'Farrell disintegrated steadily.

In May 1972 George Best rocked the football world by announcing his retirement from the game. He flew to Spain, hid in an hotel with his bedroom door locked, and pondered his future.

Just as suddenly as he had announced his retirement, Best said he would like to start training again for the start of the next season. O'Farrell fined him two weeks' wages and allowed the rebel Northern Ireland star to return.

A crisis looms

Meanwhile, O'Farrell bought Martin Buchan from Aberdeen for £130,000 and Ian Moore from Nottingham Forest for £200,000. Wyn Davies and Ted MacDougall, two powerful strikers at Manchester City and Bournemouth, were drafted in when the team began to wobble at the start of the 1972–73 season.

Manchester United were rock bottom of the First Division after a shattering 5–0 defeat at Crystal Palace in December. Six days before Christmas, O'Farrell was sacked.

Many critics deplored the way O'Farrell had spent wildly on recruiting forwards, while the defence was leaking like an old boat. His management of the men was under fire, too. Denis Law remarked: 'He came a stranger and went a stranger.' Sir Matt was not amused either: 'The Second Division was staring us in the face. The team had lost all fight. There did not seem to be a close enough relationship between manager and players.'

Not for the first time in their history, Manchester United were facing a crisis.

Chapter Four

Doc's Medicine

TOMMY Docherty had managed Chelsea, Rotherham United, Aston Villa, Porto F.C., and the Scotland team before he landed the plum job in football, Manager of Manchester United.

The Doc, flamboyant, outrageous, always snapping off a quote, remarked once: 'I have had more clubs than Jack Nicklaus.' On hearing that Manchester United's pint-sized Scottish international forward Lou Macari had escaped injury in a car accident, the Doc grinned: 'He got away with it because he was thrown into the glove compartment.'

It took Docherty less time than it takes to buy a ticket and press through the turnstiles at Old Trafford to discover what was wrong with the club. The defence needed strengthening, and he needed new blood right through the club. O'Farrell's parting words had suggested United needed to spend £1 million to win the Championship again.

He was not far wrong: in the following months the Doc chased around the country

Tommy Docherty – the 'Doc'.

with a bulging cheque book, ready for opening in some motorway lay-by in a series of cloak-and-dagger transfer operations.

Ted MacDougall was sold to West Ham for £170,000; Best and Charlton retired; Law was given a free transfer; and new recruits George Graham, Jim Holton, Lou Macari and Mick Martin pulled on the famous red shirt for the first time as Doc chopped and changed to rebuild the club from top to bottom.

The end of a glorious career

The enigmatic Best returned briefly in the Autumn of 1973. The waif-like figure was bloated; the sharp, burning pace had lost its edge; and Best had too many skeletons in the cupboard to consider renewing a career on strict, disciplinary lines. 'Looking back and being honest I must admit I didn't really want to go back to football,' he said. 'I'd had enough, my leg hurt and I knew I couldn't get back to where I was. I don't know why I went back.'

George Best's glorious career at Old Trafford ended when he was left out of a Cup-tie against Plymouth. He watched racing on the television inside the stadium rather than support his team-mates. He had a drink with the team after the match, and when all the players and staff had gone, Best walked round the empty stadium thinking of the good times he had enjoyed. He stood in the centre circle with a thick Manchester night closing round him, shed a few tears, and walked out of the ground for the last time.

Docherty wrote at the time: 'George Best has flown forever as far as Manchester United is concerned . . . He broke the back of the training that was designed to help him to peak fitness. Now all the repair work is being undone as he wastes the greatest flow of natural talent there's been in modern soccer.'

Best was to play more football for Fulham and in the United States, but the genius that had stoked-up Manchester United crowds to untold levels of hero-worship had gone forever.

Losing and winning

Meanwhile, Docherty was still poaching new players. He signed full-back Stewart Houston, midfield expert Jim McCalliog, and striker Stuart Pearson. Brian Greenhoff, Gerry Daly and Sammy McIlroy burst into the senior team from the reserves, yet results went from bad to worse as the 1973–74 season unfolded.

A black day in April 1974 cost United their First Division status. They were relegated in a game against Manchester City. Denis Law, once a United idol but now in the sunset of his career at Maine Road, sent United into the Second Division with a cheeky back-heel. Law had never experienced a sadder moment.

The match ended with Manchester United's moronic hooligan following invading the pitch.

'Don't worry, we'll be back quickly' roared Docherty defiantly. Few words uttered in football have been more prophetic.

Manchester United took the Second Division by storm in 1974–75. The club led the table from start to finish, drawing record attendances wherever it played. It lost only seven games all season to a chorus of 'Che sera, sera, whatever will be, will be' from terraces draped in red and white. Pearson, the £200,000 buy from Hull, struck 18 goals and Macari, Willy Morgan, the captain, and Daly ran an enterprising midfield.

United reached the semi-finals of the League Cup and might have gone all the way had they not met Norwich on a good day. The experts reckoned that United's all-attacking policy would crumble against the more solid First Division defences, who would absorb punishment and then hit United on the break. Not for the first time, United's critics were left red-faced. United were third in the First Division in 1975–76, a tribute to the success of a youngster the Doc had bought from Tranmere by the name of Steve Coppell.

Alf Ramsey, the England manager, had discarded wingers to win the World Cup 10 years before. Here was Docherty launching his First Division campaign with *two* wingers.

Coppell ran fluently down the right touch-line, and £70,000 import from Millwall, Gordon Hill, dazzled defenders down the other wing. Doc's demons were playing so well that supporters began to talk of Manchester United winning the League and Cup 'double', a feat only achieved by two clubs, Spurs and Arsenal, at that time.

The winning goals from Hill, the wizard winger the Stretford-enders called 'Merlin', sent highly-fancied Derby County crashing to defeat in the F.A. Cup semi-finals – and United were through to their first Wembley appearance since the European Cup exploits in 1968!

The club lost its way in the League, but surely it would not blow its chance to win the Cup for the first time since 1963? It was playing against Southampton, a team considered rank outsiders for the trophy.

Sammy McIlroy and Steve Coppell dazzled Wembley with their skills but United could never hit the form that had carried them through a highly successful season. Seven minutes from time Bobby Stokes, a good, solid professional with none of the pedigree of the stars around him, planted the winner past the diving Alex Stepney.

No Championship, no Cup . . . But Manchester United returned north from Wembley to a welcome normally reserved for winners. Docherty was King!

Public success

In two seasons Docherty had re-built the team, come close to winning the League and Cup, suffered relegation, and toasted promotion. His major signings had been a success: Coppell, Forsyth, Hill, Houston, Macari and Pearson all winning international caps. Brian Greenhoff, converted to defence, was playing solidly and soon to be joined by his brother, Jimmy, from Stoke in November 1976. Martin Buchan – cool, commanding, and a regular in the Scotland defence – captained United in 1976–77 with the promise that his team would grab silver by the end of the season.

The players swept all before them in reaching another F.A. Cup Final, this time facing the might of Liverpool at Wembley. If they couldn't beat homespun Southampton the year before, what hope this time? Pearson and Jimmy Greenhoff did the damage, cracking a tough Liverpool defence twice, to set-up a famous 2–1 victory. No prouder man than Docherty has lapped the pitch at Wembley, with the trophy held proudly in salute to fans who had roared Manchester United to victory.

Personal problems

The Doc's tears of joy were to turn to those of sorrow, only two months after the bumper champagne banquet held at the Royal Garden Hotel in London to celebrate United's fourth F.A. Cup Final victory in history.

Docherty was sacked sensationally on 4 July 1977, after announcing he was leaving his wife Agnes to live with Mary Brown, wife of the club's physiotherapist Laurie. United claimed 'breach of contract', but the Doc preferred to put it this way: 'I have been punished for falling in love. What I have done has nothing to do with my track record as manager.'

His personal life had cost the Doc dearly. Supporters said he had been fired unjustly. Manchester United, clearly embarrassed by the affair, could not see how Docherty could preach good disciplined behaviour to young footballers if he was breaking the rules.

Colorsport

Above: **The 1909 F.A. Cup Winners.**

BBC Hulton Picture Library

Above: **Billy Meredith, United's outside right, playing against Queens Park Rangers in the first-ever Charity Shield game in August 1908.**

BBC Hulton Picture Library

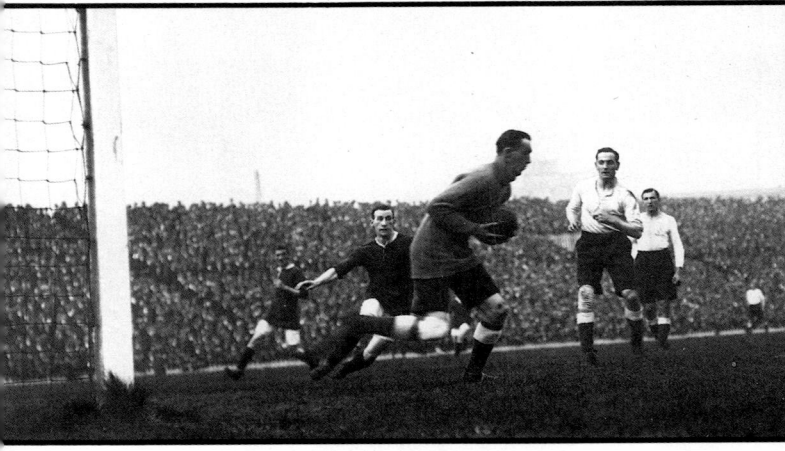

Above: **Spurs save against United at Old Trafford in 1913.**

Below: **United completed a hat-trick of F.A. Youth Cup wins by defeating West Bromwich Albion at The Hawthorns on 30 April 1955. Among the team were Busby Babes Duncan Edwards (back row, extreme left), and – front row, from the centre, L to R – Eddie Colman, Wilf McGuinness and Bobby Charlton.**

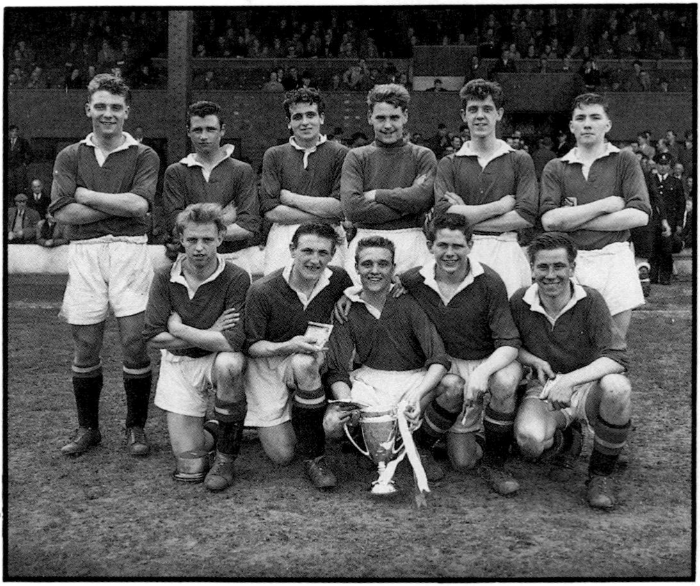

Colorsport

Colorsport

Colorsport

Right: Duncan Edwards, tragically killed at the age of 21.

Above: Matt Busby leads out the Busby Babes to play Aston Villa in the Cup Final. L to R: Busby, Byrne, Berry, Blanchflower, Wood, Foulkes, Charlton, Taylor.

Syndication International Ltd

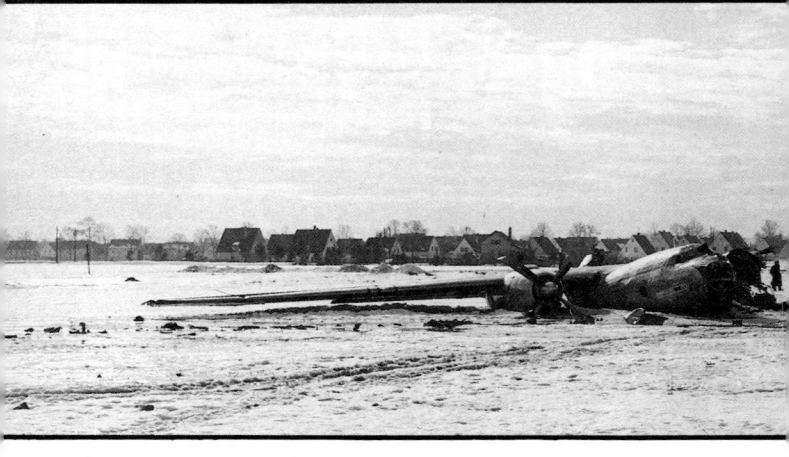

Above: **The wreckage of the crashed plane at Munich, 6 February 1958.**

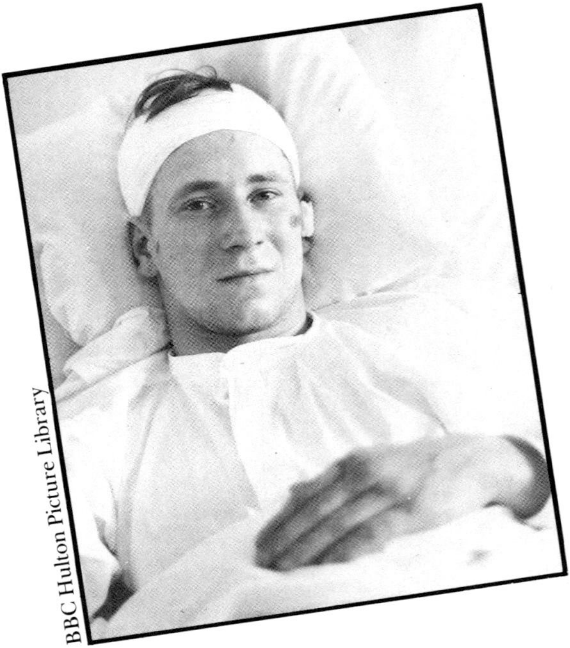

BBC Hulton Picture Library

Above: **Bobby Charlton recovering in hospital after the crash.**

Colorsport

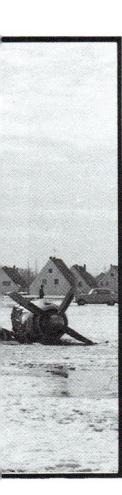

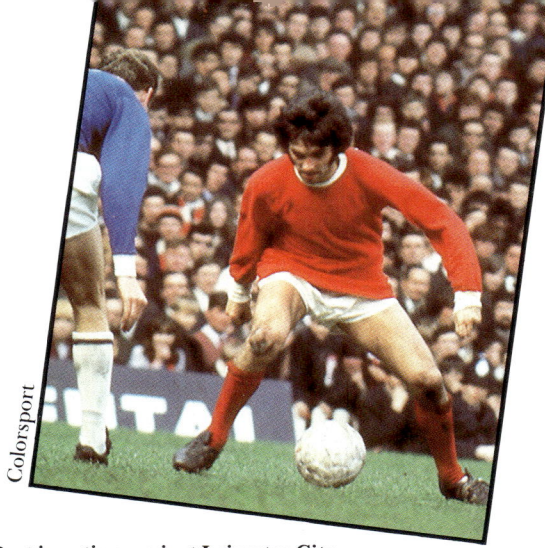

Above: **George Best in action against Leicester City.**

Below: **Winners of the European Cup, 1969. Back, L to R: Foulkes, Aston, Rimmer, Stepney, Gowling, Herd. Centre, L to R: Sadler, Dunne, Brennan, Crerand, Best, Burns, Crompton (trainer). Front, L to R: Ryan, Stiles, Law, Busby (manager), Charlton, Kidd, Fitzpatrick.**

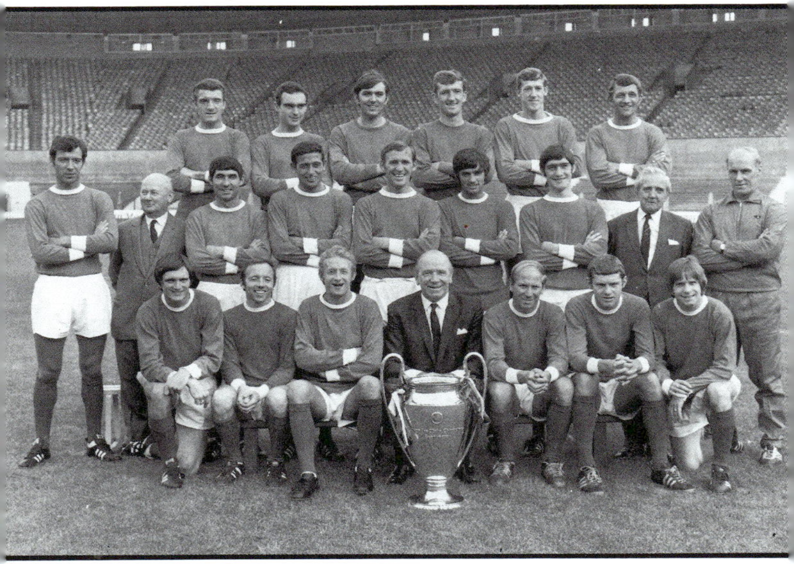

Colorsport

Bob Thomas Sports Photography

Above: **Bobby Charlton in action.**

Below: **Steve Coppell playing against Everton.**

Colorsport

Colorsport

Above: A typical salute
from Denis Law to the fans in 1971.

Below: Bryan Robson swings into action.

Colorsport

Colorsport

Colorsport

Above left: **Viv Anderson outpaces Chelsea's Kerry Dixon.**

Above right: **Brian McClair (second from right) in action against Chelsea at the start of his record-breaking 87–88 season.**

Colorsport

Above: **Norman Whiteside heads the ball in the 1985 F.A. Cup Final against Everton.**

Sexton and 'Cold Trafford'

Ten days after the Doc's farewell, Dave Sexton left his managerial seat at Queen's Park Rangers to join United on 14 July.

Sexton was recognised as one of Europe's best coaches, and one of Britain's brightest young managers. He had built two fine teams at Chelsea and Loftus Road, a feat recognised by the Football Association who were to ask him to manage the England Under-21 team and run the F.A. School of Excellence at Lilleshall in later years.

But if the Doc was extrovert, dial-a-quote, lovable and shocking, Sexton was the opposite. He struggled to come to terms with the demand for daily statements from his office for a media feeding hungrily off any morsel of news to come out of Old Trafford. He was quiet, studious, thoughtful, and believed that team affairs were private, not for public ownership in newspapers. The 'open' United had become a cold, unfriendly club.

But Sexton knew his football. He signed Joe Jordan and Gordon McQueen from Leeds United for a transfer fee of almost £1 million, and the free-running style of Docherty's side gave way to a more cautious approach under Sexton.

Mickey Thomas, a £300,000 recruit from Wrexham, helped United reach the F.A. Cup

Final again in 1979, this time losing 3–2 to Arsenal from the last kick of the game.

Ray Wilkins, one of the First Division's most creative midfield players and an England star, joined United from Chelsea in the 1979–80 season, a campaign which saw them run Liverpool close for the title.

The 1980–81 season was to see storm clouds gather above Old Trafford yet again. Sexton's teams were not popular, their 4–4–2 formation allowing none of the freedom given the great United players of yesteryear. The most famous ground in England was called 'Cold Trafford'. United were out of Europe, knocked out of the domestic Cups, and not setting the First Division alight. They were safe and unspectacular.

Something had to happen. It did. Dave Sexton was sacked in April 1981. No wonder some people were beginning to wonder whether Matt Busby had put a gypsy curse on the hot-seat at Old Trafford after his retirement a decade earlier.

Chapter Five

Big Ron's Revival

BRIAN Clough was seen by many as the perfect manager to revive the flagging spirits of a team that had lost its magic. But once again the 'Cloughie for United' campaign failed to get results.

Instead, Manchester United's Chairman Martin Edwards went for Ron Atkinson, considered then to be one of the best young managers in the country for his efforts in making West Bromwich Albion a fighting force in the First Division. Big Ron signed a three-year agreement and on 9 June 1981 held a press conference to tell the world of his appointment.

Always relaxed in the company of sportswriters and broadcasters, Atkinson said: 'When I was offered this job I was both thrilled and flattered, but I could not help feeling that Manchester United and Ron Atkinson were made for each other. It doesn't bother me that I was not the first choice. I prefer to think that I was offered the job in front of the best manager in the

Ron Atkinson – manager from 1973 to 1977.

country – Brian Clough. I will not be just United's manager, I will be an ardent fan. If the team bores me, it will be boring supporters who hero-worship the players. I will not allow these people to be betrayed.'

Atkinson injected the charisma and electricity that had been missing during the Sexton years. The newspapers called him 'Mr Bojangles', a light-hearted reference to his apparent interest in gold body jewellery. He thought nothing of cracking open a bottle of champagne at the slightest excuse. He thought BIG. He acted BIG.

Transfers and sackings

Atkinson's swoop for West Bromwich Albion's England midfield star Bryan Robson shattered the British transfer record. He bagged his man for £1.8 million in October 1981, and promptly invited Robson to sign a contract in front of a vast crowd at Old Trafford before a League game.

Not satisfied with that transfer coup, Atkinson took iron man Remi Moses from the Hawthorns also, to bring his spending to more than £2 million. By the time he had signed John Gidman from Everton, Frank Stapleton from Arsenal, and Arnold Muhren, the Dutch master from Ipswich, Atkinson had increased his spending to £3.5 million.

Atkinson was ruthless in his efforts to sweep away the trappings of the Busby, Docherty and Sexton eras. Faithful backroom staff like Harry Gregg, a survivor of the Munich air disaster; Laurie Brown the physiotherapist; youth team coach Syd Owen; and reserve team trainer Jack Crompton were sacked. 'This was a big job, perhaps the biggest and toughest in the game. It was vital I had my own men around me to give me a sporting chance of success' explained Atkinson.

Protocol and the Princess

Manchester United finished third in the table at the end of Atkinson's first season. In his second they reached the Milk Cup Final, only to lose to Liverpool.

But they had had a taste of Wembley and in May 1983 won their first major trophy under Atkinson when they beat Brighton in a replayed F.A. Cup Final. The United captain Bryan Robson remarked at the time: 'At United, there is a feeling that we still owe it to the memory of the Busby Babes to keep the team battling for cups and major honours.'

Robson, in his joy at climbing the 39 steps to receive the trophy at Wembley, broke protocol. When Princess Michael handed him the F.A. Cup, he was wearing a hat! A United supporter had planted a silk cap on his head

– and Robson had forgotten to remove it. 'I thought for a long time about writing to Princess Michael to apologise for my slip, but if I'm ever lucky enough to meet her again, will make my apologies.'

A few months later Manchester United were back at Wembley, again as winners, this time beating Liverpool in the annual clash of the Champions, The Charity Shield. Bryan Robson scored both goals in a comfortable 2–0 victory as United showed imagination and flair that augured well for the 1983–84 season.

Inspired by Robson, United gave Liverpool a fright in the race for the League title. The 'Red Devils' had not won a Championship since 1967 but the commitment, flair, and talent was there to climb to the top of the tree.

Everything went well in the League until the final furlong when injuries to Robson and other leading players caused United to lose shape and momentum. They claimed just 10 points out of a possible 30 and as Atkinson said: 'We just handed that Championship to Liverpool on a silver platter.'

The prospect of winning the League had compensated for disappointment in being shot out of the Milk Cup and F.A. Cup by Third Division opponents Oxford United and Bournemouth.

And not even the legendary Argentinian Diego Maradona could prevent United from beating mighty Barcelona to reach the semi-final of the European Cup Winners' Cup.

In memory of the Babes

Manchester United's exploits in Europe in the 1983–84 season revived memories of their titanic battles in Europe under Matt Busby two decades earlier.

United trailed Barcelona 2–0 in their explosive first-leg battle at the Nou Camp Stadium.

Just under 60,000 supporters jammed into Old Trafford for the second-leg on Wednesday, 21 March 1984. The deficit was reduced 25 minutes into the game when Ray Wilkins propelled a corner into Barcelona's penalty area. Graeme Hogg, who had scored an own goal in the first-leg, flicked the ball to Robson, and the United captain plunged through the Spanish defence to plant a diving header in Barcelona's net.

Just after half-time Wilkins and Robson combined again to put United two up, and moments later Norman Whiteside set up Frank Stapleton for a third goal.

Mark Hughes was lucky not to concede a penalty when he fouled Alonso, and United were through. Supporters cascaded onto the

Old Trafford pitch to carry Bryan Robson shoulder high to the dressing rooms.

Up above the pandemonium, hidden from the glare of the floodlights, Bobby Charlton, one of the original Busby Babes and a hero of United's 1968 European Cup win, was dancing a jig of joy on his seat in the directors' box.

Big Ron reflected later: 'The immense joy resulting from that famous victory surpassed anything I have experienced in the game. It was even better than winning the F.A. Cup.'

The semi-finals followed – and a battle with the Italian giants Juventus. Old Trafford was charged with the same electricity as it had been for the visit of Barcelona when Juventus arrived for the first-leg on 11 April.

What a line-up Juventus paraded: Claudio Gentile, Antonio Cabrini, Gaetano Scirea, Marco Tardelli, World Cup winning hero Paulo Rossi, French genius Michel Platini, and the magnificent Polish striker Zbigniew Boniek.

'Run your guts out, lads' was Big Ron's message in the dressing room. He knew it would need a miracle for United to reach the Euro Final – Robson, Wilkins and Muhren were missing through injury and suspension.

Alan Davies, playing his first game since breaking a leg, levelled the score after Rossi's shot had been deflected past Gary Bailey by the luckless Hogg. Frank Stapleton hit the crossbar in a tremendous performance by the depleted red ranks, and United went to Italy for the second-leg on level terms.

Manchester United soon trailed to a Boniek goal, but the big Northern Ireland star Norman Whiteside came on as substitute for the injured Stapleton to crack a tremendous left footer into the Juventus net. That was the first goal the Italians had conceded on their own ground in the competition that season.

Extra-time was a distinct possibility with United looking fitter and stronger, but fate was to deliver a cruel blow in the 89th minute of normal time.

A long clearance from defence fell to Rossi, and before United could recover he had scored and the European dream had ended.

Juventus went on to beat the Portuguese club Porto in the Final. It left Atkinson to consider what might have happened if he had had a full squad available for that epic semi-final battle. 'It proved to our supporters that Manchester United are once again one of the most celebrated clubs in Europe' said the Old Trafford boss.

All change

A gripping season, which left United trophy-less, had seen the club's younger players make rapid progress. Graeme Hogg, Paul

McGrath, Alan Davies and the young Welsh striker named Mark Hughes were all beginning to blossom.

But could Manchester United hang on to their captain and inspiration, Bryan Robson, the player dubbed as Old Trafford's new 'Duncan Edwards'? Juventus were particularly keen to sign the England captain. The fans mounted a 'Robson must stay' campaign, and their angry chorus of 'Are you listening Atkinson?' said it all.

Ray Wilkins, Robson's England team-mate and an inspirational player in United's midfield since his arrival from Chelsea, was the one to go, sold to AC Milan for £1.5 million. Wilkins, elected 'Player of the Year' for his outstanding contribution to the 1983–84 season, slipped quietly out of Manchester for a new life in the land of spaghetti as a small Scot arrived in a blaze of publicity.

Manipulating the money from Wilkins' transfer, Atkinson grabbed the flame-haired Scottish international Gordon Strachan from Aberdeen, and plucked Jesper Olsen from the famous Dutch club Ajax. 'Olsen will be a revelation in the First Division' said Atkinson, who had watched the little Dane tear England to shreds in a European Championship qualifying match in Copenhagen.

Lou Macari, a firm favourite at Old Trafford, was given an emotional send-off in a testimonial game against his old club Celtic before he went into playing retirement, and subsequent management at Swindon Town.

Manchester United launched their 1984–85 campaign with Mark Hughes as spearhead. The young Welsh striker was drafted straight into the first team from Central League and Youth team football, in a bold gamble by the manager.

Olsen and Strachan were joined by new recruit Alan Brazil, who had enjoyed an outstanding career at Ipswich but had endured a miserable time at Spurs.

It was not the proven thoroughbreds who were to make an impact, however, but the dark-haired, brawny Welsh tank Hughes. He scored 25 goals in 55 games that season and was voted the Professional Footballers' Association's Young Player of the Year.

No player capitalised on the speed of Olsen and the trickery of Strachan more than Hughes as Manchester United crushed Newcastle 5–0, West Ham 5–1, Arsenal 4–2, Aston Villa 4–0 and Stoke 5–0. This was the devastating football Big Ron had promised on his joyful arrival at Old Trafford!

Trials and triumphs

The club made a solid, if unspectacular start to the new season, drawing their first four League games, but by Christmas were looking impressive even though they had crashed 5–0 to Champions-elect Everton in October.

Once again, however, a promising season was to end in disappointment. Any hopes Manchester United cherished of winning the title probably perished in a tragic incident against Coventry in January 1985. Bryan Robson crashed into Old Trafford's advertising hoardings in charging through Coventry's defence and was stretchered off with a dislocated shoulder. Despite treatment, the injury was to cause him problems right up to, and during, the World Cup Finals in Mexico in 1986.

Meanwhile, United were doing well in the F.A. Cup as the League hopes faded. The club beat Bournemouth, Coventry, Blackburn, West Ham, and smashed Liverpool in a gripping replayed semi-final, going on to meet Everton in the Cup Final.

Everton, conquerors of United in the Milk Cup that season, had won the Championship and were in search of an incredible treble after clinching the European Cup Winners Cup. Saturday, 18 May 1985 saw Wembley jammed to the rafters, with tears, joy, and a match that made football history.

Manchester United and Everton were locked in scoreless stalemate after 77 minutes when Kevin Moran, United's Republic of

Ireland ironman defender, sent Everton's England midfield star Peter Reid crashing.

The tackle looked clumsy more than deliberate, but referee Peter Willis reached for his notebook. No player enjoys the shame of being cautioned in a Cup Final. But Kevin Moran was not merely cautioned. He was sent off – the first player in history to be dismissed in an F.A. Cup Final.

The incident triggered one of the bravest performances in Manchester United's long and glorious history. The team went on the attack. Norman Whiteside made a long run down the right, outflanked Pat van den Hauwe, and let rip a curling shot that bent into Everton's net past an astonished Neville Southall.

Manchester United 1, Everton 0 . . . The big scoreboard flashed the scoreline that was to see United win the F.A. Cup for the sixth time in their history.

Once more Bryan Robson collected the trophy while Kevin Moran suffered from the F.A. ruling which prevents players sent off in a Cup Final from receiving a medal on the day. Many observers at the game felt Moran had been treated unfairly. Football fans rallied to his side, sending a stream of letters to the F.A. The City of Manchester even went so far as to send a letter of protest to the referee.

The end of the Atkinson era

Football writers were reaching for their record books again at the start of the 1985–86 season. United had stormed to the top of the table with 10 straight wins. One more would equal Tottenham's record, but United drew at Luton.

Not until 9 November did the club suffer its first League defeat, at Sheffield Wednesday; but one defeat in 16 games was considered title-winning form.

Could Ron Atkinson's team capture the one prize that their fans wanted more than any other trophy and break the Merseyside stranglehold on the title?

Manchester United were to win only seven times in their next 23 games as Mark Hughes went into catastrophic decline after announcing he was joining Barcelona at the end of the season. He rattled in 10 goals in his first 15 League games, but as his worshipping fans demanded that he stay, his form fell away. He was to score only two more League goals after his brilliant start.

A crippling run of injuries was another factor in the club's slump to fourth place in the table by the end of the season. No fewer than 25 players wore a first team shirt, with the loss through injury of Bryan Robson and other key players a major factor. Pint-sized Terry Gibson arrived from Coventry in an exchange deal involving Alan Brazil, but the injury hoodoo was soon to end his season prematurely.

Hughes gave the fans a final reminder of his explosive goal-scoring talents in the last League game of the season at Watford.

Six League defeats by the end of September gave Manchester United's manager a major headache at the start of the 1986–87 season. By Guy Fawkes night, Old Trafford was in turmoil as reports began to circulate that Atkinson was to be dismissed. The following day, 6 November, chairman Martin Edwards confirmed the rumour. Atkinson had paid a heavy price for a poor start to the season and revelations about his private life. Once again a Manchester United manager had failed to emulate Sir Matt Busby.

It begged the question: could anyone follow the Great Man?

Chapter Six

Fighting Fergie

ALEX Ferguson became Manchester United's eighth manager since the Second World War after the most expensive sacking in British football history. Informed sources said that the club parted with £100,000 when they compensated big Ron Atkinson.

'Fergie' arrived with an impressive track record in management. After taking over as manager of Aberdeen in 1977–78, he guided the club through its most successful decade. He was treated with so much respect in Scotland that he was appointed caretaker manager of the national team after Jock Stein's sudden death just before the 1986 World Cup.

Ferguson was a man with a mission. He had turned down the Scotland job on a permanent basis, plus a chance to boss Spurs, and also one of the most prestigious appointments in Scotland, manager of Rangers. The size of his task at Old Trafford was illustrated fully to him when he watched his new team

**Alex Ferguson – restoring Manchester United
to its former glories?**

slump to a 2–0 defeat at Oxford two days after his arrival.

Tough times ahead . . .

Lesser men than Ferguson might have regretted the move from the outset. A few days after meeting his new players, United were involved in a £7000 wrangle over non-payment of fees for treatment to the injured Remi Moses in an Amsterdam clinic. Then the club's accounts revealed a £1.5 million deficit on transfer deals; but Fergie was already beginning to whip the club into shape. He launched a new training programme, which was carefully designed to cut down the number of injuries.

Ferguson soon began to turn a losing team into a winning one. It beat Queen's Park Rangers, and on Boxing Day went to Anfield and beat Liverpool 1–0 on the strength of a Norman Whiteside goal.

But this was to be no fairytale start to Fergie's Manchester United career. The team finished 11th in the League at the end of the 1986–87 season, and was swept out of the Littlewoods Cup by Southampton, and the F.A. Cup by Coventry, who went on to win the trophy.

The loss of Mark Hughes and his explosive goal-scoring talents was a serious setback to Manchester United's chances of winning silverware. They simply did not score enough goals in Ferguson's first season in charge. Peter Davenport, who had joined Manchester United from Nottingham Forest in March 1986, was leading scorer with 14 league goals. Second best was Norman Whiteside, who had spent a great deal of his season performing in United's midfield.

Ferguson did the double over Liverpool by beating them 1–0 at Old Trafford through a Davenport goal, but it had not been a happy month for the manager, whose pocket was lighter by £500 after the F.A. imposed a fine on Fergie for swearing at a referee in a League game at Luton. His season ended with the shattering news that goalkeeper Gary Bailey, strongly tipped to succeed England goalkeeper Peter Shilton, was retiring at 28 because of a knee injury.

United desperately needed strengthening. Frank Stapleton, John Sivebaek, and Peter Barnes had been freed, but United had not enjoyed the best of luck in the transfer market after they had failed in their bid to sign Peter Beardsley from Newcastle in May 1987.

United will be great again!

However, Fergie would not be put off in his efforts to restore the club to its former glories. He signed England defender Viv Anderson from Arsenal for £350,000 and went chasing Celtic's prolific striker Brian McClair, who had led Scotland's goal-scorers in 1986–87 with 35 Premier Division strikes. A massive £2 million price on McClair's head halted Fergie in his tracks but he continued to chase the top Scot, who had once been on Aston Villa's books, finally taking him to Old Trafford in an £850,000 deal in mid-summer.

The cheque-book was waved again in the 1987–88 season when £800,000 persuaded Norwich City to part with its powerful 28-year-old defender Steve Bruce.

That deal, in mid-season, plunged United's bank balance into the red, but chairman Martin Edwards promised to make more money available for players. 'We are just two players short of being a great side, capable of winning the title,' said Edwards, who watched the team put in a forlorn chase for the title behind Liverpool, but show encouraging signs towards the end of the 1987–88 campaign. 'I am determined to make Manchester United great again,' said Edwards.

Ferguson was spending almost as much time with the youngsters as he was with the first team squad in his second season. He had always admired the club's youth system and was determined to blood youngsters from the nursery teams as they had done in the glory days of Busby. 'We must reverse the trend that has stopped really outstanding young-sters from coming through the ranks since Mark Hughes, Clayton Blackmore, Graeme Hogg, Norman Whiteside and Billy Garton made the grade,' said Fergie.

Manchester United's high riding position behind Champions Liverpool at the end of the 1987–88 season was not good enough to meet Alex Ferguson's demands at the end of his second season at Old Trafford. But he was satisfied with the progress made by his two big recruits, defensive strongman Steve Bruce, tipped to win England honours, and sharp-shooter McClair, United's leading scorer at the end of a great début season for the club.

Fergie had become battle-hardened to dis-appointments by the time Norman Whiteside rocked Old Trafford by announcing he wanted to leave the club.

Whiteside had been ever-present in the first team since making his League début at the age of 17 against Brighton in April 1982. No player had been a better clubman than big Norm, who had flitted between a striking role and an anchor job in midfield to suit Fergie's demands. His transfer demand in February 1988 was a blow to the manager's attempts to build his own team in the way Docherty, Sexton and Atkinson had con-structed their teams in the past decade.

Achieving an ambition

Only the best players, the very best would be good enough for Fergie in his attempts to shape a team capable of winning the Championship for the first time since 1967. He knew that with the influx of two or three star players, he would have a team capable of achieving that ambition.

Bryan Robson, capped 59 times by England before the start of the 1987–88 season, had overcome the injury hoodoo that blighted his early career at Old Trafford.

Paul McGrath, born in Ealing on 4 December 1959, missed four months of the 1987–88 season through injury, but he remained the Rolls-Royce of First Division defences, arguably second only to Liverpool's Alan Hansen.

Brian McClair, who had scored more than 20 goals by the end of March 1988, was clearly a match-winner if Fergie could find a striker to help him up front. Many United fans reckoned that a McClair/Mark Hughes strike partnership would be a lethal Championship-winning combination; but would the big Welshman return to Old Trafford after Barcelona had loaned him to Bayern Munich during the 1987–88 season?

Remi Moses, locally born, was a vital part of United's midfield when fit. If he could shake off his injury problems, he would be a force in any title challenging outfit.

Alex Ferguson would need time to achieve his ambitions. Would he be given the time and the money to build the team he wanted?

Nothing was certain at the end of the 1987–88 season, but Manchester United history is so rich in triumph and disaster that anything is possible at the most famous club in the world.

Chapter Seven

Golden Greats

Duncan Edwards

THEY called Duncan Edwards 'The Colossus', an exciting mix of Rambo and an SAS stormtrooper on a deadly mission with all guns blazing.

Duncan, arguably the greatest all-round talent produced by Manchester United in their long and proud history, died at the age of 21 after the Munich Air Disaster.

When the rescue team pulled his shattered body from the wreckage of the aircraft carrying the Manchester United team, the world prayed for his survival. But he died later in hospital. His loss was the biggest single tragedy in English football; but Duncan had achieved more in his short lifetime than most players produce in a normal career lifespan.

Born in Dudley, Worcestershire on 1 October 1936, Duncan made his League début for Manchester United against Cardiff City in April 1953 at the age of 16. A year later he had won a place in the England

Under-23 team. At the age of 18 years and 183 days he became the youngest player to wear a full England shirt. When he died, he held an incredible tally for a young man of 18 England caps.

Had Duncan survived the disaster, expert observers of his trail-blazing exploits believe that he would have gone on to win a record number of England caps; more even than Bobby Moore, England's 1966 World Cup hero, who made 108 appearances for his country.

Duncan was the cream of an élite group of young footballers immortalised in the 1950s as the 'Busby Babes'. They were the product of the Manchester United youth system, fashioned and masterminded by the legendary Matt Busby, who managed the Old Trafford club from 1945–69.

Matt Busby, knighted for his genius in steering Manchester United to world-wide recognition and now President of the club, remains passionately loyal to the brilliant youngster he nurtured from schooldays. 'Duncan Edwards was then, and has always remained to me, incomparable' he says.

The secret of Duncan Edwards' remarkable progress from schools' player to a fully-fledged member of England senior team was his tremendous physique, a shrewd football brain that was way beyond his tender years, an extraordinary ability, and incomparable zest for the game.

He tackled like a tank; worked like a Trojan; and could score goals from amazing distances. He was the TOTAL footballer who would have commanded a £3 million price tag in today's transfer market.

England followers still remember his great goal against West Germany when he took possession of the ball near the centre circle, swept round two opponents, and let fly to send the ball streaking into the net from fully 30 yards. It was hardly surprising that German newspapers applauded Duncan's awesome firepower with rave headlines. Even today they remember the United starlet as 'Boom, Boom'!

Duncan scored 19 goals for Manchester United in his tragically short career, his last goal coming on 1 February 1958 in a 5–4 win at Arsenal.

Wilf McGuinness, a Busby Babe and close friend of Duncan's, has the last word on this incredible player.

'There were some hard lads around in those days who would try to hurt you. They never hurt Duncan because they never caught him. He was perfection.'

Bobby Charlton

ALMOST 20 years after he retired, Bobby Charlton remains one of the three best known footballers in the world.

He shares the stage with Pele, recognised as the greatest player in the history of the game for his remarkable performances for Brazil, and the current wonderboy Diego Maradona, who destroyed England almost single-handedly in the 1986 World Cup before lifting the trophy in a victory salute for his native Argentina.

No Englishman has made a greater impact upon world football than Charlton. 'Who do you think you are – Bobby Charlton?' has become a favourite catch-phrase for anyone commenting on some park player's efforts to shoot a goal from 30 metres, or waltz round an entire defence in a tight dribble.

And only Sir Matt Busby is more closely associated with the name Manchester United than Charlton, who played 106 times for England, wore Manchester United's red shirt on 606 occasions, and won every honour in the game.

Born in Ashington, County Durham, he joined Manchester United as a junior and signed professional forms in October 1954. His pace, ball control, and powerful shooting earned him early promotion to the famous Busby Babes line-up. No player grew up

**Bobby Charlton – played 6o6 times for
Manchester United.**

more quickly than Bobby Charlton, who survived the wreckage of the crashed plane at Munich to be thrust firmly into the limelight as Manchester United recovered from the disaster.

He represented his country at all levels: England Schoolboys, Youth, Under-23 and at full international status. He scored 49 goals for his country in an England career which began against Scotland in 1958, and ended against West Germany in the 1970 World Cup Finals. He crowned a brilliant international career by scoring the two goals to destroy Portugal in the 1966 World Cup semi-finals.

England's famous victory over West Germany in the Final was the greatest moment in Charlton's career. Few who witnessed the game at Wembley or watched on television will forget Charlton's face when Geoff Hurst cracked his hat-trick goal to sink the Germans 4–2 in extra-time.

He wept with joy.

His big brother Jack, the centre-half in England's World Cup winning team, remarked: 'What is there left to win?'

Bobby replied: 'Just one more thing, Jack.'

He meant the European Cup, a prize that had eluded Manchester United. For Charlton, it symbolized his respect and love for those Busby Babes who had died at Munich.

His chance to achieve this last ambition burned brightly in 1968 when Manchester United met Benfica in the European Cup Final at Wembley. He scored twice in United's victory, the first from a header which continues to amuse him in his role today as a director of the Old Trafford club. 'Heading wasn't exactly the strongest element of my play. I left that to others like Denis Law and George Best,' he grins.

Sir Matt Busby, who nurtured Charlton through youth teams to see him blossom into one of the world's greatest players, is never at a loss to talk of his protégé. 'There was no more graceful sight on any soccer pitch in the world than Bobby Charlton going forward, seeming to glide past opponents. There is no man who dummied or changed direction better, no man better with the long pass or the short. There was no thrill greater than when he struck that ball for goal.'

Awarded the OBE for his services to football, there is no player more respected than Bobby Charlton.

Denis Law

HE was skinny. He had a squint. And he was the obvious target for any bully wanting someone to shove around. But the weediest looking boy in the world, the son of an Aberdeen trawl-erman, grew up to become 'The King'.

There were two Kings in those days, Elvis Presley and Denis Law. Law earned *his* tag from the Old Trafford crowd for the royal performances he gave for Manchester United in a brilliant career.

Law was the first British player to salute the crowd whenever he scored a goal. Today, they all shoot up an arm if they score a goal. Law did it as if he was some sort of Emperor demand-ing recognition for his efforts.

Law was dazzling. Not a tall player, he could leap like a salmon, high above defences, to power goals with his head. And given a sniff of an opening, he would seize his opportunity to destroy defences in a few breathtaking strides.

No other player scored as many miracle goals as Denis Law. His favourite trick was to launch himself into scissor-kicks to send the ball on the volley over his shoulder, past some shaken goalkeeper.

He launched his spectacular career at Hud-dersfield Town where he drew early interest from Manchester United. Busby offered £10,000 for him, but Huddersfield manager Andy Beattie laughed at the cheek of the sum, and Law eventually went to Manchester City and on to Torino.

The young Scottish striker's life in Italy was miserable from the start. He never settled, and it wasn't long before Manchester United splashed out £115,000 to sign him in August 1962. 'I knew at first sight I had the most exciting player in the game' remarked Busby. 'He was the quickest-thinking player I ever saw, seconds quicker than anyone else. He had the most tremendous acceleration. He headed the ball with almost unbelievable power and accuracy.'

That last particular feature of Law's play had come from hours of practise in his mother's kitchen. He would fix a paper ball to the clothes rack and spend hours leaping high to head the ball.

Law made 55 appearances for Scotland between 1959 and 1974, the majority of them as a Manchester United player. He soon made his mark at Manchester United, scoring one of the three goals that sank Leicester City in the 1963 F.A. Cup Final. In harness with George Best and Bobby Charlton, he forged a match-winning partnership that was to make the trio feared wherever they went.

No striker did more than Law to help United win Championships in 1965 and 1967, but cruelly, injury was to rob the great Scot of playing in the 1968 European Cup winning team.

*

Law held the Scotland goal-scoring record for many years before Kenny Dalglish equalled his 30-goal achievement. It took the Liverpool man 97 international appearances to achieve his target. Law did it in 55.

Today, Denis Law is one of the BBC's top radio broadcasters. Who would have thought that that weedy looking Scottish schoolboy would one day become a household name hailed by the Stretford Enders as 'The King'?

George Best

ONE day in 1961, Bob Bishop, Manchester United's chief scout in Belfast, saw the boys' team he ran destroyed by a 15 year-old forward. Bishop observed at the time: 'The lad had the physique of a tooth-pick and the pallor of a child raised on chip butties.'

Bob Bishop rang Manchester United's manager Matt Busby. The conversation was straight to the point. 'Matt, I think I have found a genius' Bishop said.

George Best was to become one of the world's greatest players over the next 10 years, a pop star figure with amazing abilities – and a capacity for self-destruction.

He was soon to become a star of international proportions, a gifted entertainer who would add 10,000 to a gate if his name appeared in the Manchester United line-up carried in the morning newspapers.

George Best was just another Irish waif testing his incredible football skills in a 'foreign' land when he arrived from Belfast.

A few days after his arrival at Old Trafford, the youngster went to see his new boss: 'Mr Busby, I am homesick and want to go back to Belfast.' Manchester United allowed him to return home despite heroic efforts of persuasion from their giant Northern Ireland goalkeeper Harry Gregg.

Matt Busby wrote to Best's parents saying he hoped the youngster would change his mind. Three weeks later George's father, Dick Best, wrote back saying: 'Mr Busby, George would like another try in Manchester.'

Best signed professional forms for Manchester United at the age of 17, at the same time as the club was celebrating their F.A. Cup triumph over Leicester City in the 1963 Wembley Final.

Four months later George Best made his début, to join Bobby Charlton and Denis Law in a trio that was to become synonymous with success. They swept all before them, winning the 1965 and 1967 Championships.

Off the field, Best had become a showbiz giant in the pop explosion that followed the Beatles' world conquest in 1963–64. Dubbed 'El Beatle', Best was different from Charlton and Law. His behaviour was erratic, and he was easily led in his private life; but when he turned up for training he was utterly and ruthlessly professional. He had a unique balance of pace, close control, dribbling skills and awesome shooting and heading powers that set him way above most ordinary footballers. 'How can a 5ft 8ins rake, weighing only 10 stone 3 pounds, hammer a football with such power?' was a question that not even Matt Busby could answer.

Best won the first of 37 caps for Northern Ireland against Wales in 1964, the last as a Fulham player in 1978.

Northern Ireland was very much a backwater nation in terms of international performances following its success in reaching the 1958 World Cup Finals. One of the tragic consequences of its failure to reach the Finals of the World Cup in the Sixties and Seventies was that its mercurial winger was never to be given an opportunity to produce his dazzling football skills for a world-wide audience.

Fortunately, Manchester United were a power in the land and no player did more than George Best to make the team the most famous club side in the world during his reign.

Wherever Best went, swarms of people followed him; friends, hangers-on, minders, boys, girls, and even old ladies. He bought a new house in Manchester which became a shrine. Coach-loads of people would arrive to see where he lived. Their intrusion into his privacy was to cause his ultimate destruction.

His astonishing, but short, career reached its zenith in 1968 when, at last, a world-wide audience saw him help Manchester United destroy Benfica in the European Cup Final. In 1965–66 Best had turned on an amazing two-goal solo performance to help blitz Benfica 5–1 in Lisbon in the European Cup quarter-finals. Now, here he was again, tormenting them at Wembley with a goal and an all-round performance of handsome proportions.

Sadly, Best began to lose the discipline necessary to remain at the top in sport. He drank at nightclubs; was photographed with a whole host of women, including a Miss World; went missing from training; once 'retired' from football only to return; and finally left Manchester United to finish his League career at Fulham.

He averaged a goal every three games in 361 League matches for Manchester United.

Matt Busby says this of his Irish protégé: 'George Best was gifted with more individual ability than I have seen in any other player.'

Steve Coppell

STEVE Coppell burst on the Old Trafford scene in the 1975–76 season under Tommy Docherty's flamboyant control.

The Doc had signed the little-known winger from Tranmere for less than £50,000 – and no player was to reward Manchester United more for their confidence in his ability than Coppell.

Born in Liverpool, the 5ft 6ins bundle of trickery made such an impact in his 35 League outings for Tranmere that a host of First Division managers were chasing his signature. But there was no doubt in Coppell's mind about which club he wanted to join.

George Best had departed the Old Trafford scene and the Stretford Enders were in desperate need of a new star to cheer. Coppell supplied them with all they demanded! Doc's young lions overran most First Division defences that season. Liverpool claimed their ninth League title, but it was Manchester United who excited the crowds.

Rothmans' Football Yearbook said this in their review of the 1975–76 campaign: 'Manchester United, who had returned to the top flight, seemed to be precariously successful on a prayer and the wing power of Steve Coppell and Gordon Hill, but their exuberant industry contributed greatly to a season

Steve Coppell – power on the wing.

87

in which there was a small but definite switch of emphasis towards attack.'

Coppell and Hill offered a steady supply line of passes to top scorers Stuart Pearson and Lou Macari that season. Coppell contributed only four League goals, but as his confidence grew he was to become one of the finest goal-scoring wingers seen for years.

Wingers had gone out of fashion – except at Old Trafford – in Coppell's formative years. England's 'wingless wonders' had lifted the World Cup in 1966 and it was still considered a risk to play out-and-out wing men. 'If they can't tackle back and help out in midfield, it's not worth playing them' was the opinion of most League managers at the time.

Steve Coppell was different. He could tackle back, he could help out in midfield, and he could get forward and lay-on goals or produce a match-winning effort himself. In short, he was the *complete* winger.

England were not slow to recognise Coppell's gifted play. He won his first cap against Italy in 1978, and went on to become a firm favourite with a succession of England managers before injury forced him into premature retirement after winning his 42nd cap against Greece in 1983.

Ron Atkinson had only been Manchester United's manager a short while when he observed: 'Coppell was an honest-to-good-ness, out-and-out grafter. He was always prepared to sacrifice the outstanding attributes of his own game for the overall benefit of the team as a whole.'

Ron Greenwood, manager of England in the 1982 World Cup, remained a devoted admirer: 'Coppell was a stable and important influence. He was small, busy and elusive, a ferret of a player who worked the whole of the right touchline.'

Coppell's outstanding career was to end tragically when the knee injury he sustained playing for his country against Hungary flared up shortly before Manchester United's F.A. Cup Final semi-final game against Arsenal in 1983. At that time he was playing at the peak of his ability. He was forced into early retirement, but his magical goals for United and England will never be forgotten.

Today, Steve Coppell is one of the Football League's brightest young managers in the hot-seat at Crystal Palace. If he brings the same determination and flair to his role in a business suit that he did to the red-and-white of Manchester United and England, the game will be richer for his dive into football management.

Bryan Robson

NO player embodies all the charisma of Manchester United's legendary greats from the past more than their current captain and inspiration, Bryan Robson.

Captain of Manchester United, and captain of England, Robson has become one of Europe's finest midfield players since bursting onto the international scene against the Republic of Ireland in 1980.

In those days he played for West Bromwich Albion. In the 1981–82 season he was to shatter the transfer record between British clubs when he signed for Manchester United in a £1.8 million deal.

Announcing to the world that he had signed Robson, the Manchester United manager Ron Atkinson said at the time: 'He is the most complete midfield player in the game. He can defend, he can create and he can inspire all around him. He is a great tackler, he is good in the air, he has a superb range of passing shots and he scores goals. He's like Duncan Edwards and Dave Mackay – a scruff-of-the-neck player. He can take over any game even when it is going against his own team. He is the kind of player who makes a good team great. He will increase considerably United's chances of winning the major prizes from day one.'

*

Bryan Robson – the complete midfield player.

Born in February 1957, Robson developed his skills with a football in fields around his home in Chester-le-Street, County Durham, a region noted for its prolific nursery of talent.

Robson's first games were played with jumpers or lamp-posts as goals. As a 15 year-old, he was considered too small for professional football, but West Bromwich Albion developed his physique with a diet of one bottle of Guinness a day!

He scored two goals in his first three senior appearances for West Brom. He won England recognition at Under-21 level, but he had a struggle to convince successive England managers that he was ready for a full cap. He made 197 League appearances for West Bromwich Albion but it was not until he moved to United that he fulfilled his true potential.

He became a driving force in the midfield at Old Trafford. He became, as Ron Atkinson says, the 'complete' player – one moment clearing danger from defence, the next sprinting late into the opposing penalty area to score a winning goal.

One of Robson's goals helped kill off Arsenal in the 1983 F.A. Cup semi-finals, but that was nothing to his efforts in the Final itself! Brighton forced a replay only for Robson to help sink the 'Seagulls' 4–0 in a one-sided Wembley replay. His contribution? Two goals.

Less than a year earlier he had demonstrated his goal-scoring prowess to a world-wide audience in Spain. Making his 20th appearance for England, he scored the fastest goal of the 1982 World Cup when he netted against France in just 27 seconds.

He won his second F.A. Cup winners' medal in 1985 when Manchester United lifted the trophy again after beating Everton.

A catalogue of injuries has cost him England caps and other rewards. He suffered a series of shoulder dislocations and limped out of the 1986 World Cup with such an injury. A special operation fixed the shoulder but he then became handicapped by hamstring pulls.

The arrival of new manager Alex Ferguson and a special training programme helped the United and England star overcome his injury problems, and no player is more determined than Robson to steer England to success in the 1990 World Cup.

'To me the English First Division is the best in the world' says Bryan Robson. 'Playing for Manchester United and belonging to the Old Trafford tradition is the fulfilment of a dream. United, I believe, is still the most powerful name in club football anywhere in the world.'

No current player has done more to enhance that reputation than Bryan Robson, a lion for England and Manchester United.

Index

94